Simple Presence

Copyright 2007 by Kati Pressman.

Printed in the United States of America.

All rights reserved. No part of this book may be used or reproduced in any manner whatsoever without written permission except in the case of brief quotations embodied in critical articles and reviews.

For information, please contact
Jester Press
P.O. Box 4177
Boulder, Colorado 80306

First printing, 2007

ISBN: 978-1-881422-20-4

Library of Congress Control Number: 2007924571

Cover Design by Lael Har
www.laeldesigns.com

For Paul, David and Hyla

Also by Kati Pressman:

SHABBOS CANDLES
THE ABC'S OF SPIRITUALITY

Simple Presence
When There Is No Place To Stand

Kati Pressman

Jester Press
Boulder, Colorado

CONTENTS

Foreword 9

Introduction 17

Simple Presence and *Improvisation* 23

Simple Presence and *Elders* 35

Simple Presence and *Feldenkrais* 45

Simple Presence and *Meditation* 59

Simple Presence and *Personal Crisis* 75

The Map 83

Epilogue 95

About The Cover 96

About The Author 97

In Appreciation 98

FOREWORD

THE DENVER POST

On December 28, 1970, a family of five persons was in a head-on collision near Dillon, Colorado. The driver of the other car was killed instantly.

Initiation

I cannot say with certainty that I "died" in the accident. It happened a few years before the work of Dr. Kubler-Ross, on death and dying, had became public. My life experiences were rooted in the physical world; my perceptions were processed through my five senses. I had never heard of out-of-body experiences.

We were eager to leave for our annual Christmas vacation; swimming in the outdoor heated pools in Glenwood Springs, a small mountain town. Silently, like the dawn patrol, we walked single file across the dry lawn to our old, but reliable Chevy, parked in the driveway. There was a chill in the air. The sky was clear, with patches of morning blue pushing against the darkness. It was 5 a.m.

Our three children climbed into the back seat; I got in the front. My husband put the suitcases into the trunk and slid into the driver's seat, and put the key in the ignition.

"Seat belts," he reminded us. There was a brief chorus of clicks; except for my son in the back middle seat, which had none.

FOREWORD

The drive out of the suburban development was slow and deliberate. Porch lights were on. A newspaper boy swaying his body side to side over his bicycle, waved to us, as we passed. A few blocks west, we turned onto Broadway, the main street. Stores were closed and tucked in; still as a picture postcard. They would open in four hours. By then, we would be near Glenwood Springs.

I reached into the paper bag on the floor and found an orange. I clawed the peel carefully; the odor of the orange tickling my nose. I broke off two sections and handed them to my husband; who took them without turning his head. Immediately, there was a push against the back of my seat. Several hands, like hungry monkeys, came through the space between the front seats. I peeled some more, dividing the remaining crescents in thirds. I satisfied my hunger with a careful gulp of hot chocolate from the thermos.

As we approached the highway into the mountains, the clouds seemed lower and closer. A few wet sprinkles of snow splattered the windshield. Within a few minutes, the flakes were bigger and wetter. I felt dizzy looking at the whirl of snow. I placed a pillow between the passenger window and my face, and dropped my head to the right until it made contact with the cool cotton. I fell asleep. Time and space dissolved.

Simple Presence

The accident happened – but not in my field of perception. I felt a shift in my body, a sense of gentle lifting into a vast space of silence; then – very swift movement toward a vortex of light. My eyes open to a face so close to mine, our breaths are breathing each other's. I feel a 'drop' into my body, now wrapped in excruciating pain. Closing my eyes, I sense a lift.

Movement thrusts forward in a narrow band of brilliant light, pulsing at its center; contraction and expansion.

My eyes open again. The face is gone. Instead: the intrusion of a large lamp with harsh, inquiring light. A weighted wrestler of pain pins me down. My eyes close again, seeking respite. Again, a strong lift into a swift current of energy, carries me forward. I discern several dim human shapes at the edge. I hear a low hum, which grows louder, then shapes into a word.

My daughter is crying, "Momma!"

This time, the 'drop' into my body is slow, fixed and final, in contrast to the gentle, whisper-like 'lift' out of my body. Both spaces were filled with light; one generating guardianship over me; the other, 'catching' me in a net of pain and fear.

FOREWORD

My eyes are wide open now. I cannot move. Someone speaks to me. "There's been an accident. You may have a broken neck." Moaning voices are coming from behind a white curtain ahead of me. "Your family is on the other side of the curtain. Everyone is O.K." The curtain is pulled halfway so I can see my family for a moment, and then pulled shut. I close my eyes, hoping for another 'lift'. There is none. My travel in the tunnel of respite is over. I sink into unconsciousness.

My daughter had a possible ruptured spleen and was flown by helicopter from Dillon to the closest Denver hospital. The rest of us were transported in one ambulance to another hospital in Denver. One son endured a broken jaw and concussion; the other, a broken nose and concussion. My husband suffered several fractured ribs and chest bruises. I fell forward hitting my neck on the dashboard, breaking the hyoid bone, which sits behind the larynx. My chin was deeply lacerated and I received compound fractures to the left wrist and forearm. Even though asleep, I had held my left arm in front of me to brace the impact. How had my arm known to do that?

Within two weeks we were all home. We became a family bonded by doctor's appointments and taxicab schedules. Our hands would seek each other, tenderly marking that we were still alive, still together. Underneath our lives, invisibly, the accident created a metaphorical fault in the grounding of our family; that eventually widened and separated us.

I have no memory of the accident. To have no recall of this most traumatic event, compounded by my inability to speak, felt intensely disorienting. Even when I could speak, six months later, no language was available in the remnants of shock. Historical patterns of behavior and identities were shattered forever. I felt disconnected, hanging onto one thought that repeated itself in a soothing whisper. "We were all alive. We were all alive." But also, "What had happened to us?" Every breath chased a question. Every question met with silence. More questions. More silence. I had stepped into a way of living without knowing; patient, expecting no answers; and eventually standing in Simple Presence.

I believe the accident – and accepting its consequences – was a preparation for engaging the four fields of energy I entered into and describe in the writing of this book.

K.P.

Simple Presence

When There Is No Place To Stand

INTRODUCTION

Dear reader:
I have something to say.
The time is now.

Global events have startled my sense of security and well-being; exploiting old fears and inviting new ones. Every day there is the possibility of succumbing to these fears and feeling powerless. There is another way. I want to share my experience of standing with troubling times; a state of mind I call "*Simple Presence.*"

Everyone knows the story of someone looking at a glass of water and seeing it half full. Someone looks at the same glass and sees it half empty. I propose that the glass of water is both. If I dwell on my glass of water as being half-full, I may be called an optimist. If I dwell on my glass being half-empty, I may be called a pessimist. In truth, half-full cannot be half-full without the glass being half-empty. They exist with each other, because of each other. When I hold both ideas together, I am neither optimist or pessimist. I am both. These perceptions melt into a third state; a non-conflicted state of non-duality.

Simple Presence

All that I know can be represented by the number of words written in this very line. What I don't know can be represented by the infinite space surrounding the words.

Most of what I seem to know, comes out of four fields of experience: improvisation training for the theatre, designing *Simple Presence* with elders in a nursing home, the Feldenkrais Method training, and meditation practice. These processes have a basic attribute in common: they bring attention to the present moment through stillness and awareness. From this position, response is spontaneous and aligns with 'what is', as it arises.

Presence is unrehearsed. *Simple Presence*, without agenda or expectation of a desired outcome, invites the possibility of a number of different outcomes. Having options is the ground for making choices. Making choices is the ground for freedom. Choosing responses that work for us, is the ground for feeling satisfaction and even joy. The moment passes through us and brings the next moment as it leaves. We can barely notice the pulse, the beginning or end of a moment.

Life can pass through us, exactly as it is, no more, no less. If we feel less, it is the foundation for complaint. If we want more it is the basis for expectation and fantasy. When we complain, our mind seems to pointing to something that is missing. We want something to be what it is not, or we want to have something that we do not have. Pulled away from the present, we may imagine some inability to handle what the moment has to offer.

Dr. Hans Selye, in his book, *The Stress of Life*, describes three components for a balanced life – stimuli, adaptation, and rest. Of these three, rest is the most crucial. If we go from stimuli and response to stimuli and response, without rest, we may soon experience stimuli and reaction, stimuli and reaction. *Simple Presence* yields that place to stand, to rest before reaction. (Why is this important? Reaction breeds reaction, globally and personally. Breaking the cycle of reaction in ourselves, we can become skilled at making adaptive responses that are called for in each moment.)

There is the joke about a woman feeling cold. Her husband is sitting nearby, reading the newspaper. She asks, "Hon, would you please get up and close the door? It's cold outside." He says nothing. She asks again, with some irritation, "Hon, would you please get up and close the door? It's COLD outside." Again, he says nothing and doesn't get up. This time she is in an angry reaction. "GET UP and close the door! It's cold outside!!" This time the husband gets up and closes the door. He says, "So now, it's warm outside?"

The woman could have closed the door herself. She could have put on a sweater. She could have taken a hot bath. She could have turned up the thermostat. If she were present to her own circumstance, she could have made the adaptive response that fit best for her, without reaction or projecting her needs onto someone else. *Simple Presence* generates effective responsibility for ourselves.

The four fields of experience I write about train for adaptive responses within the context of their unique field. In theatre improvisation, there is playing in the moment for an audience; in the nursing home, being with 'what is' for the elders, in the Feldenkrais training I learned to 'listen' to the patterns of movement in the body of the client before I moved a part of the body, and finally *Simple Presence* taking root through Vipassana meditation practice.

Simple Presence is the common sense of our spirit: a skill that enables and empowers people to meet any circumstance as it occurs in the moment. It is the posture of balance. Balance restores the economy of energy. Our world is lop-sided in its expenditure of energy; destructive rather than restorative. Our energy and balance seems depleted on every level, spending ourselves in *reaction*. *Simple Presence* can be expressed in every interaction; in the way we cut a vegetable or speak to people, watch a man walking his dog or meet the challenge of crisis.

We have forgotten that we are born with *Simple Presence*. Watch a baby being present to whatever grabs its attention in one moment and the next. Watch a mother watching her baby, without story, without naming.

We can experience power over, power within, and powerlessness. Power over suggests control and a potential for the use of force. Power within suggests containment and equanimity. I hope to seed the empowerment of *Simple Presence* in the reader, to intoxicate the reader with *remembering* their power within; and to dissolve the fear of powerlessness as we meet the accelerated crisis of deep change.

Simple Presence
and Improvisation for the Theatre

*Eighty percent of life is just
showing up. The other twenty
percent you make up.*
~ Woody Allen

Fall, 1969

I cut the ad out of the newspaper. It read: "Improvisation for the Theatre. Have fun while learning. Classes begin in two weeks. Call...". *Have fun while learning?* It seemed perfect timing for a perfect invitation. I was experiencing near burn-out working as an R.N. on the Crisis Unit of a psychiatric hospital in Denver. I signed up for the classes.

After ten weeks of training, six of us, three men and three women, were recruited to form a semi-professional theatre improvisation company called "The Works." We performed in various venues around Denver for two years.

Training went further than developing skills for performance. We became a family; building trust with each other so that we could support and be supported in taking risks on stage. Away from the stage, every interaction became the curriculum for improvisation. The moment became a playground for practicing attention and awareness.

What is improvisation about?

The intent of the improvisation "Theatre Game", as created by Viola Spolin, is a set-up; giving the player an opportunity to respond from the unrehearsed mind, in the moment, without thinking.

Simple Presence

I am reminded of a story about a young actor, out of work for a long time who finally lands a bit part in a play. His line is: "Hark! I hear the cannons boom!" He rehearses it night and day. He writes it on his walls. He practices different emphasis on each word.

The night of the play he puts his make-up and his costume on and steps onto the stage at his cue. Comes the sound of the cannon's boom. He jumps and says: "Jeez!! What the hell was that?"

This is how most of us live our lives. We rehearse our roles and our lines, and the moment of reality startles us.

Improvisation training is about accessing the unrehearsed mind to make spontaneous responses that are adaptive to any given circumstance. That is, to 'fit' the context of the circumstance. It is training for spontaneity within a structure. The rules of the improvisation game are the structure. Imagine a dog on a very long leash. You can let the dog move within the whole measure of the leash. If you let go of the leash, (let go of the structure) you may have spontaneous behavior from the dog, but it may also run away.

One of the favorite audience participation games in improvisational theatre is "First line – last line." The audience calls out a first line, and a last line. Let us say, the first line is: "Now, where did I put the box?" The last line is: "I can't do this anymore." A player steps forward and mimes looking for a box, and says: "Now, where did I put the box?" and continues to establish the context of the scene. "With all these boxes and only a candle to see with, how am I supposed to find the one with the pillows for the King?" The player has established context for the scene. The context is accepted by all the other players as a current reality. Each player who steps into the scene, responds to what has been presented, building the scene to conclusion, where it makes sense for someone to say the last line: "I can't do this anymore." The by-product of focusing on scene-building is a loss of *self*-consciousness. Once the actor has stepped into a scene, she cannot leave the stage until her part is finished. Accepting what is presented in the scene, acceptance of another person's world, *even if it is made up*, creates an environment for unrehearsed, intuitive responses that complete the scene.

Improvisation trains us to respond in non-habitual and spontaneous ways to the set-up of the game. The game can unfold in any number of ways. Anything goes, as long as the response is within the structure of the game. The improvisational actor is present and still in the moment, allowing the spontaneous response to come through the front door, so to speak. This does not necessarily mean a quick response, but a response that occurs without trying. It just happens.

It takes courage to hang out with a feeling of uncertainty in the here and now, without a referent, relying on intuition for an adaptive response that moves the scene forward; in life as well.

It is impossible to live to without habitual responses. Habits begin innocently. For example, if you enter a classroom for the first time and can sit anywhere, you will probably pick out a chair that suits your first preference. Each time you come into the class, you sit in the same chair. It becomes "your" chair. Notice your reaction if someone is sitting in "your" chair.

A preference became a habit.
A habit became a pattern.
A pattern became a perception.
A repeated perception became a belief.

Improvisation cuts through habits, patterns, perceptions, habits, and lands the player in the moment. There is nothing else.

Sept. 1974

I did not imagine that improvisation skills would be useful in my work as an R.N. on the crisis unit of a Denver hospital. I was working the night shift when these skills presented an alternative possibility of dealing with a crisis.

Billy, a Vietnam veteran, became violent this night. Two police officers and his roommate had brought him into the crisis unit. In the lobby, Billy ran behind a billiard table, blocking the three men. He held a billiard cue-stick like a spear with one hand, while his other hand rolled a billiard ball on the table. All the while he screamed obscenities. The three men were yelling at Billy to give up the cue stick and billiard ball, threatening him with injury if he did not.

I entered the lobby from an adjacent ward, alerted by the sounds of yelling. Standing in the archway, I grasped the scene in an instant. Billy turned to me, startled. His eyes focused on mine. We were caught in stillness and surprise. He and I stared at each other, the room quiet during the momentary pause. I opened my hands, inviting Billy, "Come with me, I'll listen." He moved slightly toward me, tentative. I walked backwards, slowly, never taking my gaze from his face. Billy followed, as if dancing, one step at a time, until we came to my office. I stepped aside, and gestured for him to go in. Inside, we sat down in chairs facing each other. Billy began a litany of anger and grief, most of it unintelligible. I listened, still but alert, with no agenda, and total acceptance.

I don't remember how long he raged. At one point, I noticed his roommate and the officers walk by the office, looking in. Finally, Billy put his head on the desk and sobbed. When he seemed subdued, I gently touched his arm. He looked up and I motioned for him to stand up. I took his hand and walked him to a hospital bed where he fell asleep.

I asked the three men to return the next morning.

Making notes in Billy's chart, I was filled with amazement as I reviewed what had happened. The responses I had made to Billy seemed to have had a life of their own, rising out of my state of surprise. This was my first real life 'scene', where my interactions had been totally improvised.

The intensity of the situation had quickly brought my focus into the moment. The words, "I will listen", was what the three men were *not* doing. It was a moment of truth: responding to what was called for.

Truth cannot be rehearsed.

The starkness of the situation, unfamiliar and intense, brought me directly into the moment. I did not know what to do but be still. Waiting until the next line occurred to me had served both of us well. I listened. Billy's resolution of his anger through his *expressing* it, was a significant lesson for me. All I did was show up, and allowed Billy to complete his rage with total acceptance.

Team playing for entertainment was one thing, but now I had experienced the deep intimacy of meeting a real-life circumstance; connecting with another being, who was separated from himself and scared. It was a direct encounter with the dynamics of *power over* (the three men could have carried out their threat, I am sure) and the potency of *power within* that I experienced with Billy.

The improvisational player, like the spiritual seeker, scans for contact with an intelligence that is beyond words; an

Simple Presence

intelligence that flows through us, organizing our body systems, running our bloody highways, beating our heart. We know it is there. We cannot name it. We can only prepare an inner environment alert for the possibility of its appearance.

Unfinished business in real life is one of the greatest source of tension and stress. Unlike other games like chess or football, where the object is to win, the object of playing Theatre Games is the *context,* not the contest. Improvisation had cultivated the seed of *Simple Presence.*

I was utterly surprised at its next manifestation.

Simple Presence

with Elders

*One doesn't discover new lands
without consenting to lose sight
of the shore for a very long time.*
~ Henry Miller

April, 1974

I had been hired to facilitate training programs for nursing home personnel. These programs were based on the psychosocial aspects of getting older. In addition, the director of the project had asked me to develop an activity program for the sixth floor residents. The sixth floor of the nursing home/hospital complex was known by most of the medical staff and more alert residents as "the place where people go to die." The challenge seemed enormous.

The elevator opened and I walked onto the sixth floor; a gallery of contrasts. The nurse's station directly in front of me, issued an antiseptic odor; the 'day room' to the right of the nurses station, smelled of a musky mixture of urine and dampness. There, about forty of the forty-four sixth floor residents sat, bent over, large sheets binding them into wheelchairs, placed randomly. A twenty-one inch color television was tuned in to a 'soap opera'. The windows were shaded from daylight to keep the glare off the television set. At the nurses station, young women in starched, crisp white uniforms were writing notes in charts. The patients also wore uniforms; faded pastel colored gowns, limp and loose, covering pencil thin bodies. The serious hum of the nurses, mingled with the emotional tones coming from the television set, presented a surrealistic scene to my mind. *What kind of a program could be developed that would make any sense to what seemed to me, to be an incoherent, disconnected situation?*

I sat down next to a woman who was bent horizontally over a tray table that supported her frail arms. *How could I reach through to her? What would catch her attention? What did she need?*

For the next three weeks, Monday through Friday, from nine to eleven each morning, I sat in the day room, quiet and alert, offering my intuition to the forty residents positioned around the television set. One Friday morning, the last day of the third week, I brought my mind into focus, meeting an edge that would not give. Hopelessness spread through my body, pulling me into its center.

I was ready to believe that a program that could engage these people was impossible. It could not be done. I did not have access to their world. I did not know what they needed or wanted.

I was giving up. My head drooped slightly. My hands opened, palms up. My mind let go of its focus. I let go of my intention of finding a program for these residents. A rising depression flowed through my body. I allowed my body to slump into the chair. I let my arms flop, noticing that my body imitated the posture of the patient. Exaggerating my depressed posture, I turned my feet on their sides, and dropped my jaw. I bent forward, my head down. I sat this way for about twenty minutes.

My back hurt. My ankles tingled with numbness. I needed to stop. I forced my aching spine to straighten in the chair, in order to sit up. The woman, small as a sparrow, who had been at my side for twenty minutes, five days a week for three weeks, without speaking, opened her eyes wide. She said, "You know, my brother was a cantor in Russia. This is what he sang to me." She then sang for me, lucid and clear. I do not know the Russian language, but it was obvious the woman did. While she sang, her eyes were open and alert. When she finished singing, she lowered her head again, bent over the tray table and closed her eyes.

For three weeks, I had sat without a response from this woman. Was it by mirroring her posture that she seemed to have connected to her own predicament? There was something else also. We had shared an experience; true. But it was more than that. We had connected in a way that had dissolved our separate identities. Our interaction was coherent and made some kind of 'sense'. The discernment I made was: we *were* the experience, not *observers* of the experience.

In my office, I reviewed what had taken place, and made notes. My unrehearsed, non-judgmental presence during the three week period seemed to have established a bridge of trust. By mirroring the resident's posture and feelings, her memories seemed to have crossed the bridge and landed in the present moment. Over the weekend I designed a program called "*Simple Presence.*" The program would be tried with four selected patients who had been non-communicative for at least two months. I would spend twenty minutes each day with each patient, with no agenda. I would not initiate or intervene in any way. The patient would be the one to initiate verbal interaction. If there was no initiation within twenty minutes, I would leave. If there was interaction, it would be over when the patient signaled it was over, by closing their eyes and silence. It was important to have every interaction with me initiate from the patient, to reinforce the feeling of their being able to control *something* of their lives. I was presenting myself with no agenda, no expectations.

When I returned Monday, this same woman had wheeled her chair to the elevator doors. Was she waiting for me? I pulled up a chair and faced her. Within a few minutes, she lifted her head. She began talking about her brother; that he was older and smarter than she. I said nothing. I was waiting to be invited to speak. She was relaxed and lucid. Then she asked me: "Do you have a brother?" I answered, "No." She smiled, nodded, closed her eyes, and bent over the tray table. The interaction was over. I moved to another patient.

When I gave up on finding a program, the program had found me. Over the next three months, every one of the four patients I had chosen, initiated interaction with me at one time or another in our daily sessions. There seemed to be an intelligence that became available from my presence, just 'being with', that fostered non-habitual expressions from the patient. After three months, I excitedly presented my report, with thoughts of the next step. I was thanked and my report was put in the bottom drawer of the director's desk. That was the end of it at that nursing home, but not for me.

Simple Presence with elders had picked me up, carried me, and dropped me into a field of mystery and intelligence that seemed more real to me at times than the physical world. This new guest in my psychology seemed to love stillness and patience. How could I sustain this level of intuition? I often sensed what was needed, but I did not know of a practice where I could access more of the mystery, or establish an opening in myself for a visit.

Sometimes all that is needed is to live the question.

Simple Presence

and The Feldenkrais Method

*God guard me from the thoughts
men think in the mind alone.
He that sings a lasting song
thinks in the marrow bone.*
~ William Butlers Yeats

March, 1984

It would be my first cross-country driving trip; from Denver to northern California. I was worried that the stress of the long trip would affect the long-standing bursitis of my right knee. My friend, Elizabeth, familiar with complementary approaches to health, suggested I see a Feldenkrais practitioner. I had never heard of the work and felt reluctant. Elizabeth offered to pay for the session if I was not satisfied. With that incentive, I made an appointment to see Anna. I described the problem to Anna, laid down on a low, padded table, fully clothed and apprehensive.

There was very little talking in our session. Anna's touch was gentle and supportive. I felt my body relax, allowing her to move my limbs and musculature as she explored the range of movement throughout my body. My mind compared the tiny and discrete movements she made with the large, definitive movements that had been made by my physical therapist. She began small movements of my left knee. I reminded her that the problem was in my right knee. She nodded and continued to move the left knee between her two hands. Puzzled, I gave up attention to my right knee and focused on whatever Anna was doing. Near the end of the session, she came to the right side of the table, lifted my right knee, moving the knee in gentle increments until it flexed and extended easily, *without pain*. I was speechless. Anna had begun her work by dropping focus on what I called the "problem" of my right knee. My mind was confused as to why she was working on the left knee. That confusion and attention to what she was doing to my *left* knee allowed me to let go of holding in my entire right side. Movements made in the left knee by Anna seemed to have sent information to my right knee about *how a knee moved*. My right knee, totally relaxed, seemed to remember past my holding it as a problem knee. The problem seemed to be in the holding, not in the knee. I had a second session the next day. Two days later, I left for California. I drove for four days without pain. In Palo Alto, I continued the Feldenkrais work with Dr. Marty Weiner.

Marty is a gifted man. I have never been able to discern whether it was the Feldenkrais Method, his remarkable talent, or his philosophical approach that worked so well for me. In truth, it did not matter; his work was as totally integrated as he was.

One time, I stopped him in the middle of a movement on my chest. I was sitting on a stool and Marty, on another stool, was sitting at my side. I asked him to repeat what he was doing. I was able to sense restriction of my ribcage because of something outside of the movement. I noticed that his *presence* to me seemed total. It was not just the discrete movements he made, but this 'being with' me that allowed my awareness of the restriction I held in my ribcage. Marty did not fix the restriction or make it go away. With exquisite, precise movements of my ribcage, he took over my holding: moving toward more restriction. The muscles around the ribcage released their tension, as he was doing their work for the moment. As my muscles relaxed, I took some deep breaths. Then Marty introduced small movements that encouraged the ribcage to expansion, inviting my breath to follow. The habitual way of restricted breathing was still available, but now there was another possibility. With presence and repetition, my ribcage could learn another pattern of breathing.

Moishe Feldenkrais said, "If you know what you are doing, you can *choose* what you want to do."

I returned to Denver in late 1985, in time to attend a Feldenkrais Workshop called Awareness Through Movement, led by Ruthy Alon.

Simple Presence

Ruthy's teaching is transmitted with joy and a deep appreciation of life and its limitations. She embodied the essence of awareness and presence in her movements and interactions. It was impossible not to be led to a direct inner experience.

Lying on a mat in a gymnasium with fifty other students, I rolled, flexed and extended parts of my body in tiny movements, slowly bringing awareness to the subtle sensations in my body. My *awareness* now attended to my entire being, regulating the movements from the soft and clear directions coming from Ruthy.

The afternoon of the last day, I felt bored as we lay on our backs and moved our legs in a variety of tiny movements. Attention was directed to the right knee, (my 'problem' knee.) After a few minutes I sensed spirals of movement within the knee and release spread over my entire spine. I felt as if I were sinking through the floor, and yet felt buoyant and light. I experienced 'how' my knee moved through ligaments, tissue and bones.

Awareness flowed through me into the room, the students, dissolving identity, merging, integrating the many and all; nothing left out or separate.

I had found the work I wanted to do and I wanted to be trained by Ruthy Alon. Her next training would be in Sydney, Australia, in the fall of 1986, a year and one-half away. That seemed like a long shot. Where would I get the tuition? Where would I get money for an airline ticket to Australia? It was so far away both in time and space. Nevertheless, I filled out an application with Ruthy and forgot about it.

My life had turned in another direction.

Summer, 1986 - INTERIM

My apartment building was being converted into condominiums. I had to move. Instead of looking for another apartment, I put my belongings in storage and accepted a job at a boy's sports camp in Maine for the summer. Two weeks before camp was over, I received a letter from Australia, forwarded from Denver. The Ruthy Alon Feldenkrais Training had space. Was I still interested? I had completely forgotten.

A few phone calls later, I knew the amount of tuition, the cost of a round trip ticket to Australia, and the total of my summer wages. I was fifty dollars short of a match.

S IMPLE P RESENCE

I had made arrangements to stay with a friend in Denver after camp. My winter clothes were in storage. All I had with me were my summer clothes. It would be summer in Sydney, Australia, when the training began. I was going to Australia.

FELDENKRAIS TRAINING, 1986

The first sessions of the training were held in a huge barn-like room, a part of the Sydney Fairgrounds. Sunlight streamed through wooden doors, the rays catching the dancing dust. I felt excited. All of the other students were natives of Australia. Conversations around me were playful and incomprehensible to my ears, rich in a song-like dialect.

Ruthy came to the front and welcomed us. We sat down on our randomly placed mats, attentively listening to her. This is how the training would go. There would be two month- long sessions each year with a two month break in between, for four years. The first two years would focus on floor work, called Awareness Through Movement; as in Ruthy's Boulder workshop. The last two years would be training for table work, called Functional Integration; like Anna's and Marty's work with me.

The floor is our first teacher. Our nervous system learns to push, crawl, stand and explore against the support of the floor. By repeating these learning processes in incremental, small steps, we engaged awareness of our individual ways of moving and using our bodies; attending to places where we did not move easily; places of holding. With awareness of *how* we do the behavior, the process becomes the curriculum. Lessons are based on unlearning habitual patterns of movement, and re-educating the nervous system to new, more efficient patterns of movement.

One afternoon, in the second session of the training, a graphic example of the effects of our holding patterns presented itself. We had been working for two weeks on a complicated series of small movements without success in completing the lesson. Ruthy began instructions for the lesson. In just a few minutes, all of us were groaning with the fatigue of failure.

I don't know if it was Ruthy's genius, or her own sense of frustration with the lesson. She stopped the instructions. There was quiet in the room. We waited. Then she said, "O.K. Everybody do the lesson as badly as you can."

There was a moment's hesitation. *Do it badly?* One of our boldest students began to twist, roll and kick. In a moment, we all followed. There was a cascade of bodies bumping

Simple Presence

into each other, laughing and whooping. After a few minutes, spent and happy, we settled on our mats. A wave of deep sighs came from everyone in the room, followed by the silence of a collective "amen." It was a holy moment. After a few moments, Ruthy began the instructions again. Every one of us completed the lesson easily. What had happened? Ruthy had given us permission to fail, which by-passed our habitual mental constructs of wanting to do it right. It was a valuable lesson.

In Rumi's poem, *Cutting Up An Ox*, the butcher is describing how he cuts.

> ...I would see before me the whole ox.
> After three years, I no longer see this mass,
> I saw the distinctions.
> But now, I see nothing with the eye.
> My whole being apprehends.
> My senses are idle. My spirit free
> to work without plan,
> follow its own instinct
> guided by the natural line,
> by the secret opening,
> the hidden space,
> my cleaver finds its way
> I cut through no joint, nor chop no bone.

It is in this spirit, that the Feldenkrais practitioner makes precise movements, in increments, efficiently touching the body and moving only what is necessary to communicate a new pattern of movement. To do that, *Simple Presence* is a requirement, so that awareness and attention can be focused.

When we incur an injury, physical or psychological, there is withdrawal of the injured part, so that healing can take place. However, after the healing has taken place, residual holding in a kind of protective stance may occur. This holding may become habitual to avoid further hurt, and leak into our thinking and behavior after the injury itself may be forgotten.

I remember a woman elder I saw in Sydney, Australia who demonstrated the tenacity of habitual holding after an injury.

Two years before, she had been in a car accident which resulted in fractures to her right hip and leg. According to her doctors, the hip and leg had healed. Her presenting complaint was that she had difficulty walking because her right leg felt stiff and "like a pole". I looked out the window as she got out of her car with great effort. She placed her hands into hand crutches and very slowly, her body rigid, walked to the door. I opened the door and gently placed my hands on top of her hands, walking backwards until we were at the work table. She turned, hands still on the crutches and sat down. She slipped her hands out of the crutches and gave them to me. I was not thinking deliberately, but placed her crutches in a corner across the room, about six steps away.

I worked with her left leg first, and found her movements soft and easy. She fell asleep, in a light doze. That isn't exactly what you want in a session, because you want the client to bring awareness to the patterns of movement. I approached her right leg tentatively, and it too, moved soft and easy. Up and down, flexing, extending. At the end of the session, she woke fully and reported: "That feels wonderful!" I helped her to stand, my hands on her elbows. She stood tall and straight, balanced on her feet. Then the miracle happened. She saw her crutches and walked in an easy stride toward them. When her hands slipped into the cuffs of her crutches, she turned around and she walked in *exactly* the same halting movement of stiffness and careful small steps as she had made at the beginning of the session! Fortunately, she did return for more sessions until new movement patterns were established.

My dance with the Mystery was quickening.

Simple Presence
and Meditation

...*words and measures do not give life; they merely symbolize it. Thus all explanations of the Universe couched in language leave the essential things unexplained and undefined.*

~ Alan Watts

Summer, 1972

My introduction to meditation occurred in the summer of 1972. I had taken a position in a residential program called, "Adventure in the Arts", teaching Theatre Improvisation to high school students at the University of Rhode Island, in Bristol.

One night after supper, I was strolling across the campus to return to my room. A group of students were walking toward the main lecture hall. Curious, I followed them and stopped outside the hall to read the posted sign: Transcendental Meditation Lecture and Demonstration - 7 P.M. I had no reference for either word: transcendental or meditation. I went in and took a seat in the back of the room so I could leave easily, if I wanted to. By the end of the lecture, intrigued by the promise of equanimity, I applied for instruction. Two days later I was instructed and initiated into the program.

I brought an apple and flower as gifts for the teacher. I sat on the floor in front of a serene, young and lovely woman. She taught me a mantra, a non-intelligible phrase. As I said the mantra to myself, tears flowed gently down my face; warmth surged through my body. I sat completely still, repeating the mantra for the next hour. I felt a sense of expansion with no boundaries.

I was hooked. This state of mind continued more or less for the remainder of the summer in Rhode Island. Perceptions were softer; time flowed easily; teaching was effortless. When I returned home, however, meditation was difficult; thoughts interrupted concentration continuously. At times, meditation was boring. But one day I experienced a shift in my body and felt connected to the threshold of my inner world. Confusion changed into inquiry; insecurity turned into curiosity; apprehension melted into trust. I continued to meditate, content in the T.M. practice. However, I had just touched the surface. In Sydney, Australia, 16 years later, on Christmas of 1986, I fell deeply into myself by beginning Vipassana meditation.

Christmas, 1986

Journal Entry

The first session of the Feldenkrais training is completed. I have been invited to spend the holidays with my friends in the training. That would be fun. But I prefer to go on a ten day meditation retreat at the Blue Mountain Retreat Center. I need some time alone. It will be good to relax and sort through what I have learned.

MEDITATION

The train ride was pleasant. Daydreams of quiet strolls down or up the mountain paths, eating wholesome vegetarian meals, meditating twenty minutes in the morning and afternoon filled me with anticipation.

The taxicab driver left me off at a dirt road pointing to the location of the center. A curtain of sprawling trees spread before me. I walked several hundred feet before I could see it. The grounds were circled in loose metal wire, fencing the plain and barren land. I stepped into an opening and walked to a large cabin in the center of the land. Mattresses lay in piles on the porch; a misty dust rising as a vapor. Young men and women were moving about quietly, carrying objects without effort.

Rotating water hoses sprayed spasms of water onto small flower beds, waking the buds to attention.

I had chosen to come up a day early, to secure my orientation to the land and the accommodations. A young woman directed me to the row of rooms set aside for women. I lay my duffle bag on a bed in the last room, closest to the meditation hall, and walked back to the main building. No one was around. I went into the dining hall to see if I could get a cup of tea. At the entrance, a large blackboard on an easel, announced:

Simple Presence

> WELCOME TO THE VIPASSANA RETREAT
> TEN DAYS OF NOBLE SILENCE
> DECEMBER 24 TO JANUARY 2
> REGISTRATION BEGINS AT 2 P.M.

Vipassana? Was that the name of the teacher? A city? When I had inquired, I had only mentioned that I was interested in a meditation retreat around Christmas. I had made an assumption that it would be T.M. because that was the only meditation I had ever heard about. And what did "Noble Silence" mean? What, dear God, had I signed up for?

The next day at lunch, my hands hugged the bowl of vegetable soup for warmth and connection. My mind swirled in confusion. I ate slowly as I listened to a young man describe the agenda for the next ten days to a group of about one hundred people in the hall.

There would be blocks of two hour meditation periods beginning at 4:30 A.M. Speaking was allowed with the manager or the teacher in the interview only. No writing. No other talking. No escape. Ten days, ten nights, a new technique to learn. I had begun my silence, noble or not, sinking into my feelings of anxiety.

Meditation

I fell asleep early that night. Huddled in layers of clothing and blankets, the chilly wind of the night grazed over my face. I prayed for deliverance and closed my eyes. Sleep came quickly. A long single tone piercing sound vibrated like a wooden mallet against my skull, jarring me awake. The sound pulsed away. Before the last of it, another piercing tone reached beyond my eardrums, dipping into my teeth. I flicked the flashlight under my pillow, guiding the beam of light to my small traveling clock. It was 4:20. A.M. Where was I? Soft beams coming from a number of flashlights illuminated rays of dust moving against dancing shadows.

I tugged my sweater and blue jeans over my pajamas, bumps of wrinkles twisting under the sleeves. I pulled my wool hat over my head. I stepped out of the room and leaned my back against the wall for support as I slipped into my boots, which were chilly and stiff. I followed the flow of figures moving in the dark toward the meditation hall. Inside, pillows and benches had been arranged in neat rows with an aisle in between. Women sat to the right of the aisle, men to the left, reminding me of an orthodox synagogue. I took a low chair near the back and wrapped myself tightly in the blanket that had been placed on the seat. Wriggling my body into the folds for warmth, I fell asleep.

Simple Presence

A resonant, loud, monotonous chanting intruded my sleep state, like screeching chalk across a blackboard. The chanting in Sanskrit continued for thirty minutes. Was it one voice chanting or a hundred? The assault of sound had awakened me. My teeth, face and head pounded with unpleasant sensations. My physical discomfort was a prelude to the inner irritations about to occur. So began my first day of Vipassana meditation.

The instructions were simple enough. "For three days, the meditation will be to simply pay attention to the breath. Do not suppress thought; gently bring attention back to the breath when you are noticing thought. Sit comfortably. It is important to sit as still as possible. This is an intense activity for the nervous system. Like focusing a laser beam of concentrated attention. If any movement is done, let it be done very slowly so as not to jar the new awareness that is being cultivated."

Without realizing, I had begun a course in advanced *Simple Presence*, one that required total concentration towards my inner being. Thoughts clamored for my attention. Presence brought me back to my breath and became a moment of pause, withdrawing all meaning from the moment.

MEDITATION

I surrender into the moment. That is all there is.
A toe is moving. Which toe?

I feel giddy. Disorientation is setting in. After an hour, there is a fifteen minute break. I get up to walk and my legs seem to move through vats of molasses. I walk slowly into the dawning sun. A patch of warmth glides over my face. I take a deep breath in release. For the moment, I feel I can do it. I hear myself saying, "Yes. Yes." I return with determination.

For the next three days, the chase of the breath is the entire curriculum. On the fourth day, we are instructed in the body scan. "Bring awareness over the body, inch by inch, left to right, right to left, head to toe and back again. When a part of the body catches attention, stay there with awareness as long as you can." Unfamiliar, but almost enjoyable phenomena occur; *eyelids fluttering... muscle twitches... lips curled in a sneer.* I cannot seem to control the movements.

The body receives the laser beam of awareness greedily. I am stopped in my body scan by an excruciating crunch in both shoulders. I get up with intention of running out of the hall, but I walk carefully. The sensation of pain melts as I walk. I return to sit and pain returns tenfold. My shoulders are blocks of fire. I surrender into pain. My shoulders begin to move in tiny spasms, growing larger. My eyes squeeze tears. My chest is shaking, trembling deep. My eyes, floating in liquid, open. I name it. *Grief, deep grief.* Tears stop flowing. My breathing falls into a sigh. Gratitude rises in my chest and throat. Years of holding buried grief are brought forth to be released in awareness.

So the days continued.

On the tenth morning when we could talk to each other, words tumbled out like a river raft going through crashing falls. My cabin mates and I hugged each other and jumped up and down in glee. We had made it!

Released from the intense concentration of ten days, my being expanded into a deep compassion for everything. Trees, the people, myself, the earth, the mountains, everything I could see and beyond – existed in one unified one field of energy. My inner world had gone past my mind to a state of *being*. Vipassana meditation had taken me deeper into myself.

Mix and Match

For the next three years of the Feldenkrais training, I would spend each Christmas break at a Vipassana Meditation retreat, in the Blue Mountains of Sydney. I graduated from the Feldenkrais training in December, 1989, and returned to Colorado. After two years of working in Denver, I moved to Boulder. I joined a Vipassana meditation group and found it to be a perfect match for my Feldenkrais practice.

As the meditation practice cultivated awareness of my inner self, I deepened awareness of the client. Energy and movement took place simultaneously between the client and myself. As I touched a pattern of movement, so I was touched. When my hands felt resistance or tightness, my hands went soft and neutral, allowing the client to feel my presence in my hands. This contact informed the client of total acceptance, and they had permission to let go of their resistance. Without the client's holding pattern, through precise repetitious movements I made in increments, the client could re-learn a new pattern. I had no agenda for what happened in a session. Every moment was fresh and new with potential.

A young man who was interested in becoming a Feldenkrais practitioner asked for some introductory sessions with me. As he lay on his side, I moved his right shoulder forward and backward gently. A question arose. "Have you ever injured this shoulder?" I asked. He was quiet for a moment, then turned and sat up. "That is amazing. I fell out off a tree when I was about ten years old, and landed on my shoulder. I wore a cast for months!"

Why I had asked that question? Had I felt the shadow of a cast in the holding? It turned out that he had long forgotten about the injury until that moment. As I rocked the shoulder gently, he remembered the fall and began to cry. For about twenty minutes, I rocked the shoulder blade; he cried quietly. The shoulder seemed to fall into my hands. He breathed a deep sigh of release.

While holding presence to the client, I was also holding presence to myself. Old fears of falling rose to my awareness, auditioning for my attention. After that session it became part of my practice to sit and meditate after I saw a client, in order to scan what had showed up for *me* in our session. The Feldenkrais method and my Vipassana meditation practice became partners in the dance of growing awareness. I experienced a more reliable reality in stillness. As old patterns arose, I remembered the phrase from Scripture which said, "It came to pass." In my mind,

I would think: "It came *in order to* pass." The value of presence, just presence to what arose, noticing the fall and rise of thoughts, was becoming a part of my Feldenkrais work.

My first winter in Boulder, I became ill with severe bronchitis. Presence and awareness were my first tools when I felt ill, right next to the pharmaceuticals. I would pray for a way to 'be with' my illness. I always sensed the same instruction. Be still. Allow. Allow. Be present to what is presented.

I was not, however, prepared for the next level of illness.

Simple Presence
and Personal Crisis

*What is to give light
must endure burning.*
~ Victor Frankl

Personal Crisis

March, 1997

The last Friday night of a Vipassana meditation retreat, we gather to hear the evening talk by our teacher. I close my eyes. He speaks of equanimity. The last thing I hear is, "Meet every circumstance with mindfulness and equanimity."

A vise cracks around my chest. Excruciating pain twists through my torso. I cannot hear or see anything. My attempt to meet the pain with equanimity is futile. No edge or contour of the pain can be found. As my chest becomes a solid wall of contraction, the force of pain expands. There is not a hair's breath of space in my body that is not in the pulsing wave of pain, the eye of the storm.

"This is it. I am having a heart attack.... Headlines read, "Woman dies while meditating"... or more believable... "BOULDER woman dies while meditating".

Twenty minutes later, I hear the sound of a small bell. The talk is over. Fully present now, I can see the teacher and hear my voice, "I need some help". Two friends crawl quickly to me (they are already on the floor). They lift me up and walk me outside into a car. We are driven to the emergency clinic. The physician on duty gives me an injection to subdue the pain and wants to hospitalize me.

Simple Presence

I refuse. I would rather be in the peace and stillness of my room at the retreat, among meditating friends, than alone in a strange hospital. I sign a release and agree to notify the doctor immediately if there is change in my condition.

Because death had not occurred in the cyclone of contraction at the retreat, I felt the danger had passed. There was something else. I felt joy, – indescribable joy. I felt whole, alive and totally present, my senses vividly active.

On Monday morning, returning to Boulder, I went directly to my physician's office. A lung scan revealed that I had had a massive pulmonary embolism that had shattered into many smaller ones. I was admitted to the hospital immediately and, for a week, it seemed I could die at any minute. A living will was made out at my bedside. My friends gathered every day in two's and three's, some singing to me, their faces full of love and caring. It seemed that my time had come for transition. I felt calm for some reason, unafraid of the possibility of death. As my friends sent cascades of love towards me, I felt a reciprocal wave of peace that went out towards every one. Every touch and exchange of words with anyone who spoke to me, was a breath of grace. The hospital staff carrying out the medical procedures were so gentle and soft with me, I thought, "Yes, I must be dying." But nothing hurt. I just kept noticing my breath...now shallow and short; now quiet and thin. *Simple Presence*, meeting the circumstance, had melted into an experience beyond anything I had ever known Dying: I felt most awake. One week later, breathing deeply and grateful to be alive, I went home.

I spent a year in the slow process of recovery. I continued meditation and cut back on my Feldenkrais practice. The call seemed to be for slowing down, pacing my work. I lived just one day at a time. Writing in my journal kept me connected to continuous inquiry; a state of wonder and question.

I did not expect any answers.

For a long while my body curved into itself, in a posture of protection. My body seemed to retract and get smaller. Most of that first year of recovery, I moved on automatic pilot. I hardly noticed how *Simple Presence* had become a part of my every day being. In this process of writing, I am recalling, imaging, feeling the experiences again as I see the words gather on the computer screen. *Simple Presence* seems to be anchored in my total being as I write. *Simple Presence* has landed in my consciousness: a place to stand. *Simple Presence*: like a membrane of intelligence, with a porous front and back, allows awareness to shift through my experience of writing. Right now.

The current of my life has flowed from an island of separateness into a larger ocean of possibility: of experience of the whole. Accepting my part in the whole, I accept the imperative of responsibility to show up and be present to my life as it occurs.

How did I get here?

Simple Presence

The Map

The map is not the territory.
~ ALFRED KORZYBSKI

THE MAP

The map is not the territory.

What does Dr. Korzybski mean? The meaning I make from that sentence is that whatever I say is *about* an experience; it is not the experience. Language can only approximate any experience. My experiences are like fingers pointing to the moon. They are not the moon.

I have described an experiential mapping of aspects of improvisational theatre, the Feldenkrais Method, work with elders in a nursing home, and meditation. Although very different in context, these activities have qualities in common that are embodied in *Simple Presence*. All begin with holding an open state of mind. An open state of mind accepts without judgment, observes without prejudice, is present without expectation.

In *Simple Presence*, one is patient for information coming beyond the mind and senses; waiting for the response that seems to be called for. In stillness, intuition can take root and flow into the interaction until a response that fits and seems most adaptive to the circumstance, seems inevitable and is expressed. When that happens there is a sense of completion and satisfaction.

Simple Presence

In theatre improvisation, the actors could feel the eagerness of the audience wanting us to create a scene that had a beginning, a middle and end. The support and permission allowed us to play and even miss the mark, until we expressed a response that moved the scene to conclusion. *Simple Presence* was the doorway to effective improvisation.

Working with the elders in the nursing home, required exceptional patience. What kept me sitting there day after day, in what seemed an impossible situation? The residents seemed to have developed a code of silence and withdrawal as a way to cope with their difficult circumstances. I was trying to access that code. The staff seemed to relate to the *diagnosis* of the resident, not the *person* with the diagnosis. The designation of the 6th floor as "the place that people go to die" was their primary context of interactions with the residents. The residents also identified the 6th floor as the place where "people go to die", before they were transferred to the 6th floor. Why wouldn't they feel hopeless, depressed and non-communicative? They had accepted the perceptions of the authorities in their lives. Yet the residents who had been diagnosed as being senile or having dementia, spontaneously spoke to me in a lucid manner. Did that happen just by my presence accepting, without judgment, what is?

THE MAP

I think so.

I believe the residents lived in a world of duality, of "us" and "them". "Us" being the residents. "them" being the staff. My hunch about the woman I first sat with, is that she seemed to have interpreted my demeanor of helplessness and depression…as a person who was like herself; one of the "us." For three weeks, I had been present to her without doing to her, or for her. I certainly wasn't one of "them". She could trust me. *Simple Presence* had accessed her code of behavior.

The Feldenkrais Method first trained the development of awareness in the practitioner. The practitioner, through non-habitual movement in a session, engaged the client in learning self-awareness. The client, as well as myself, was learning something about perceived limitation and the power of awareness, in re-learning. It was the non-habitual movement done ever so slowly that evoked awareness. As I moved a part of the body of a client, I was being moved also. Awareness is the natural expression of *Simple Presence.*

The most potent point of *Simple Presence* is that its energy is expressed as power within: not power over, which is expressed as force. Energy against something or somebody generates force; energy that is being with what is, evokes power in its stillness.

In my practice of meditation, thoughts, images, and sensations are ever-changing. They are frequently representations of something else, something deeper, something more hidden and unavailable. When I focus with *Simple Presence*, meditation can go deeper.

I believe that *Simple Presence* is available to everyone in varying degrees, with different experiences than mine. With that said, I propose an underlying theory for my experience of *Simple Presence*. Consider the following, as *if* it were true.

Scientific explorations confirm that there are fields of energy beyond our perception; influencing every interaction we make as human beings. What I am suggesting, is the possibility that we can connect with those invisible fields of energy when we are in *Simple Presence*.

Simple Presence is more about being rather than doing; allowing rather than expecting; accepting rather than efforting.

Two fields of energy occur simultaneously in all of us. The one that we present to the world is mostly rehearsed, masked and habitual. The inner field, often hidden from ourselves, influences our perceptions of reality. We flow back and forth between these two fields, from memories of the past and plans for the future. What is real?

Moving between the two, we are mostly airborne; landing on our feet, in our truth, is a long shot. However, if we can be present in the moment, grounded in the present reality of our lives, we can live the truth of what is, live through the truth of what is, instead of avoiding it, and move on.

I am not a scientist. In my work in theatre improvisation, with elders, the Feldenkrais method, something beyond my intuition, allowed unexpected responses, which felt real and true to me. That state can be repeated so that spontaneous responses can occur; in different contexts.

The universe is a unified field of energy. The configuration of thoughts, sensations, images that flow through my body, is not separate from that field of energy and is an integral inter-dependent part of the whole. Any interaction or movement in the whole affects every part. Any interaction or movement in a part affects the whole.

Simple Presence

When I perceive myself as separate, knowing boundaries, where you begin and I begin, where God is located, I limit my experience. Limiting my experience may generate a feeling of security and control. What is happening *there* and to *them* is distanced in an illusion of separateness.

Adaptation to a constantly changing reality is tricky. Not only that, but every moment has happened a mili-second before we can perceive it. Not only *that*, but every interaction has myriad of influences upon it, from the past to the present. As soon as you say something *is*, it changes. The motion picture of our life, a fast track of our perceptions, is accepted *as if* our world is so. We may feel stable and secure if we count on things being solid and permanent. They are not.

Interruption and change are in full throttle in today's world, both man-made, and from the forces of nature. The particular quality that makes human life manageable is our ability to adapt to the stimuli of our experience. If we feel cold, we can put on a sweater or turn up the heat. The range of stimulus in a stable, unchanging environment is not very large. We have resources and can make choices for a small range of experiences.

THE MAP

Today we are faced with vast, biblical circumstances. We cannot pretend we are separate from anything that happens in our world. How can we adapt to a world that is in chaos? How can we meet the unraveling of every form of security we may have known.

I believe *Simple Presence* is the portal allowing the unified field of energy that I suppose, to inform us. The moment is all there is, because it is constantly creating and changing. If we hold *Simple Presence* to our experience without reaction or labeling, *we* may be created and changed. To be able to show up and be with the accelerated changes in our lives, is the only security we have. *Truly.*

Simple Presence is a place to stand.

EPILOGUE

A recent retreat I attended, ended with a dharma talk on intention. I was deeply touched and left the room and moved into the dining room as if carried by a great wave of feeling.

An early snow that morning tumbled over the trees and bushes. My gaze was pulled to one leaf. One leaf, capped in glittering snow, bowing, as if in gratitude.

Out of my own stillness, in that moment, came a thought. What if – in these tender times – people all over the world – not out of fear, not out of anger, *intended* and engaged in *Simple Presence* to what is ?

Could we become *that* still ?

Anything is possible.

ABOUT THE COVER

The "yud" is the smallest letter in the Hebrew alphabet. It is complete in itself with no parts. It is not insignifcant, however. The "yud" is essential to and is in the formation of every other Hebrew letter. It is considered to represent the metaphysical. Its numerical value is ten.

Lael Har, the artist, has skillfully combined the essence of *Simple Presence* and the mystery and power of the "yud" by placing two facing each other; as a representation of possibility.

In real life, *Simple Presence* evokes energy that is beyond words, that flows between any number of worlds of perception; transforming the experience of difference into an experience of no boundaries, no separation.

ABOUT THE AUTHOR

Kati Pressman is an elder, retired R.N. and Feldenkrais practitioner. She has been a college teacher, nurse educator, workshop facilitator and improvisational actress. Her first professional writing was for Channel 7, Denver, Colorado: *Beyond Bingo*, a television documentary about people who were active and alert in their elder years. Her poem, *Initiation*, won first prize, with over 76,000 entries in a national contest sponsored by Montel Williams in 2000, in support of research for muscular dystrophy.

She says: "I have been writing since I was a teen-ager, delighted with words and their magic in making meaning. When I was very young, coming home from school, I would walk backwards sometimes, to see where I had been. When I returned to walking forwards, I noticed that the path remained the same. What I saw depended on where I looked. This habit led to a tendency to see things differently. Or was it the habit of seeing things differently that led to my walking backwards? I don't know."

Simple Presence is an invitation; to a way of seeing things differently in a traumatized world of fragmentation and insecurity; to remember who we are really; and to not be afraid.

In Appreciation

I am grateful to my dearest friend, Gloria Kubel, valiant warrior, who ,years ago, gave me a package of typing paper for my birthday, and encouraged me to write. She still encourages me, but I buy my own typing paper now.

I am grateful for every event and person that presented the challenges and blessings that have impacted my inner life; opening me to deep self-inquiry.

~ Kati Pressman

To Order copies of
Simple Presence

Write to:
>Jester Press
>P.O. Box 4177
>Boulder, Colorado 80306

Please enclose:
>$12.00 for each book plus $3.00
>for shipping and handling

**Attention:
Care-givers, Educators, Organizations**

Discount is available for bulk orders.
For more information:

Write to:
>Jester Press
>P.O. Box 4177
>Boulder, Colorado 80306